# THE JUDGEMENT OF PARIS

JILL DUDLEY

PUT IT IN YOUR POCKET SERIES
ORPINGTON PUBLISHERS

*Published by*
Orpington Publishers

*Cover design and origination by*
Creeds, Bridport, Dorset
01308 423411

*Printed and bound in the UK by*
Creeds


© Jill Dudley 2016

ISBN: 978-0-9553834-8-9

# THE JUDGEMENT OF PARIS

The Judgement of Paris triggered the Trojan War. It all started when King Peleus of Phthia married Thetis, the daughter of Nereus, a kindly sea-deity whose home was a cavern deep in the Aegean sea. Their wedding was a great affair to which all the gods and goddesses were invited.

One person had not been invited to the wedding, however, and that was Eris (Strife or Discord). In a fit of pique she came anyway and, in order to stir up trouble, cast down amongst the guests a golden apple on which was written 'for the fairest'. Aware that this would cause a controversy at the wedding, Zeus, supreme god of the ancient world, instructed his messenger-son Hermes to take the apple to Mt. Ida, a mountain range in the region of the Troad in north-west Asia Minor. There Paris, the son of King Priam of Troy and his wife Hecuba, would be the judge as to who was the 'fairest' between three goddesses.

Before giving birth to Paris, Queen Hecuba had received a warning in a dream that the child to be born would bring about the destruction of Troy. As a result the baby was abandoned on Mt. Ida where it was suckled by a she-bear. On finding the baby still alive after five days, a shepherd took him home and reared him as his own. So it came about that he grew up to be a shepherd on Mt. Ida.

The three goddesses to be judged by Paris were Hera, goddess of women and marriage, Athena, goddess of war and patroness of arts and crafts, and Aphrodite, goddess of love. All were beautiful in their own immortal way, and each offered Paris a bribe in the hope of being chosen. Hera's bribe was power over all the known world, Athena promised him victory in battle, and Aphrodite offered him the most beautiful woman in the world. Although Paris was already married to Oenone, a nymph on Mt. Ida, he was young, handsome and virile, and had no hesitation in handing Aphrodite the golden apple.

Despite the Judgement taking place on Mt. Ida, he was also by this time, or soon afterwards, reconciled with his real parents who had forgotten the dream, and he lived in his own house near the palace. In due course Aphrodite, true to her word, saw to it that his father sent Paris on a mission to King Menelaus of Sparta. There Paris was made welcome and, at a banquet held in his honour that evening, he met the king's wife, the most beautiful woman in the world. Aphrodite must have smiled when she saw Helen's gaze meet his, and the flame of passion ignite between them.

Helen* was the daughter of Tyndareus, king of Sparta, and his wife Leda. It was said that Lord Zeus had been enamoured of Helen's mother and had turned himself into a swan to ravish her; it was suggested that Helen had been the result of this union and, somewhat unusually, had been hatched from an egg.

Whatever her true parentage, while Helen's husband was called away to arrange the funeral of his grandfather in Crete,

Paris became her lover. In no time he had persuaded her to run away with him. Not only did he steal the king's wife, but he also took a quantity of Spartan treasure.

It was an intolerable abuse of King Menelaus' hospitality, a breach of etiquette, a slur on the king's honour. His wife seduced by the King of Troy's son? It was an impertinence, an international scandal! With his wife gone (and valuables gone with her) Menelaus turned to his brother King Agamemnon of Mycenae* for help.

Immediately the terms of Helen's marriage swung into action. Before she had married, her father had arranged a contest for her hand to which numerous eligible suitors had come from all around Greece to compete for her. They displayed their skill in wrestling and athletics, and underwent tests in toughness and endurance in the hope of winning the prize of the king's beautiful daughter. Furthermore, as there could be only one winner, Tyndareus had made them all swear an oath that the lucky one who won Helen would be supported if asked by all those who had lost. So it was that, in obedience to this oath, King Agamemnon managed to gather a considerable army of warrior kings and nobles who, under his supreme command, set sail across the Aegean for Troy with the sole purpose of retrieving Helen.

For nine years battles raged on the Trojan plain with excessive bloodshed and loss of life suffered by both sides. Homer's epic poem the *Iliad* is concentrated entirely on the tenth year of the war. In that year Achilles,* the son born to King Peleus and Thetis, and the finest warrior in the Greek army, suddenly laid down his arms and refused to fight. He was incandescent with rage that his lovely slave-girl, Briseis, had been taken from him by King Agamemnon because his own captured slave-girl had turned out to be the daughter of a priest of Apollo and had to be returned to her father.

From her cavern deep under the sea, Thetis heard her son lamenting his loss, and crying out to her from the seashore where the Greeks had beached their ships in Beşik bay. She now lived separately from her husband since he had caught her trying to immortalise the infant Achilles by placing him in the embers of a fire one night. Her husband's anger and lack of trust in her divine powers had prompted her to leave him and return to her cavern under the sea. Another story about how she had tried to immortalise Achilles was that she had held the infant by the heel and immersed him in the river Styx. Where she had been holding him remained for ever mortal and, therefore, vulnerable, hence the saying 'Achilles' heel'.

Seeing now how wretched her son was by the loss of his lovely slave-girl, Thetis agreed to go to Lord Zeus on Mt. Olympus who owed her a favour. When the other gods had found him over-bearing and had rebelled, Thetis had called on Briareos, the hundred-handed giant, who was able to calm things down. Because of the part she had played then, she thought Zeus would repay her now and agree to give help to the Trojans until such time as Agamemnon was prepared to return Briseis.

Thetis did as she had promised, and from then on with Zeus' support the Trojans began to advance and push the Greeks back across the Trojan plain to their ships. When they started to set fire to the fleet Patroclus, Achilles' lifelong companion, could not bear Achilles' sulking inactivity, and implored Achilles to let him at least lead their men, the Myrmidons, into battle. Achilles relented, and gave him his armour to put on – armour which the god Hephaestus (god of fire and a master craftsman in metal work) had given his father as a wedding present, who in turn had given it to Achilles when he set off to war. Achilles also gave Patroclus two immortal horses, Xanthos and Balius, (also a wedding gift to his father from the gods), together with his charioteer Automedon. He believed the Trojans, seeing Achilles' armour and horses, would take fright thinking he had returned to the fight.

Patroclus fought with great courage killing many men, but he himself was soon to be killed. Apollo, who supported the Trojans, stood behind him and ...*striking his back and broad shoulders with the flat of his hand, he made Patroclus' eyes spin and knocked the helmet off his head*...(Iliad 16:791-792). While he was still stunned, a Trojan wounded him but quickly drew back amongst his men, and it was King Priam's eldest son Hector who delivered the coup de grâce with his spear. He then stripped him of his (Achilles') armour. Even Achilles' immortal horses went into mourning for Patroclus, their heads down, with hot tears dropping from their eyes, and their manes hanging to the ground.

On learning that his beloved friend was dead, Achilles was grief-stricken. Again his mother Thetis came up from the sea to console him. This time she promised to go up to Mt. Olympus and ask Hephaestus to make him a new set of armour.

When the new armour came, Achilles lost no time in putting it on and going in to battle. He would not rest till he had avenged his friend's death and killed Hector. He was the swiftest of all warriors, and had, amongst other things, been trained in warfare by the wise and learned Chiron, a centaur, into whose care he had been put after Thetis had returned to her cavern in the sea.

On seeing Achilles back on the battlefield, the Trojans were panic-stricken. King Priam, watching from the citadel, saw his men fleeing in terror back to the city, and immediately ordered the gates to be opened to allow them back to safety. Hector, however, stood his ground and faced the swiftly approaching Achilles. But, as he drew near, he himself lost his nerve and fled. Three times they circled the walls of the city, and on the fourth Achilles aimed and drove his spear through Hector's throat. He then tied his body behind his chariot, whipped up his immortal horses and galloped around the city walls dragging the body behind, before returning with it to the Greek camp.

He showed no mercy. And yet that evening when King Priam arrived with a wagon-load of treasure and implored him to return the body of his son so he could give him the proper funeral rites, Achilles was gentle with the old man, and agreed to do what he wished. He knew what it was to grieve for a loved one. So an eleven days' truce was allowed for King Priam and his family to mourn Hector, and on the twelfth the battle was resumed.

Homer's epic poem ends here, and it was left to later writers to explain what happened next. Achilles was eventually to be killed on the battlefield. His death was caused by Paris himself who fired an arrow at his heel which was guided there by Apollo. Later, Paris also was killed.

The final fall of Troy was vividly described by the first century B.C. Roman poet Virgil in his *Aeneid*. Aeneas, son of Aphrodite and Anchises, a shepherd on Mt. Ida, escaped from the burning city, and related the whole pitiful story at a banquet given by the queen of Carthage. He described how first the Greek hero Odysseus* masterminded the idea of the Wooden Horse* which tricked the Trojans into thinking it was a gift for Athena to appease her for the earlier theft of her *palladium* (an ancient image of the goddess which had fallen from heaven and was believed to protect the city). The Greeks left the Wooden Horse (this gift to Athena) on the Trojan plain, and sailed away, fooling the Trojans into supposing they had gone home. Instead, they were hiding behind the nearby island of Tenedos.

King Priam and his people were overjoyed at what they thought was the end to the conflict. There were great celebrations, and the Wooden Horse was brought into their city and placed before the temple of Athena.

That night the Greek fleet sailed back, and the thirty or forty hand-picked warriors concealed in the Wooden Horse emerged from their hiding place, having been released by a spy they had managed to infiltrate into the city. They killed the sentries on duty, flung open the gates and the Greek army entered the city. The sleeping Trojans were soon awakened by the screams of the dying, and the noise of crackling wood and falling masonry as the fires took hold and the city blazed.

In the midst of the inferno that followed, the hapless King Menelaus entered a house intending to slaughter all the inhabitants inside, and saw Helen in the shadows, with the light from the burning city illuminating the room. His first emotion was rage and exhaustion because of all the death and mayhem resulting from her adultery. He raised his sword to kill her, but Aphrodite intervened.

One story claims that Helen lowered her garment to reveal her naked beauty, another that she drew her veil across her face in a seductive gesture; yet another story says she threw herself at his feet and clasped his knees in supplication and sorrow at what she had done. In all events, Menelaus was suddenly overcome by love, and his sword dropped from his hand.

Such were the consequences of the Judgement of Paris. The blame for such bloodshed could be laid at the door of Aphrodite, goddess of love. Or it could be said to be the fault of Helen who threw away home and family for a passionate relationship. Or it could be blamed on Paris for accepting the bribe of the most beautiful woman in the world and forgetting he already had a wife.

Whoever was at fault, the beautiful Helen, having left a trail of disaster in her wake, returned to Sparta with her long-suffering and forgiving husband and, as far as is known, they lived happily, or at least reasonably contentedly, until their deaths.

For over three millennia their story has been told and retold. The Judgement of Paris, which had set it all in motion was sung about by poets; it was painted by artists on pottery-ware; it was later written about by playwrights and acted out in dramas. And still the story lives on. It was a scandal which the goddess of love brought about by malicious design. The Judgement of Paris brought with it terrible tragedy; it brought the early death of the enamoured lover, and yet somehow, Helen came out of it unscathed. But then, when all is said and done, she was the daughter of Zeus – she was not just the most beautiful woman in the world, she was divine.

*\* Denotes a separate booklet on the subject.*

# GLOSSARY OF GODS AND HEROES

ACHILLES – Son of King Peleus and Thetis, a minor sea-goddess. When she tried to immortalise the infant Achilles by plunging him in the river Styx, she held him by the heel which remained for ever vulnerable, hence the 'Achilles' heel' saying.

AENEAS – Son of Anchises and Aphrodite.

AGAMEMNON – King of Mycenae, and brother of King Menelaus of Sparta.

ANCHISES – A shepherd on Mt. Ida. He was loved by Aphrodite and they had a son, Aeneas.

APHRODITE – Goddess of love. In the Trojan War she supported the Trojans.

APOLLO – Son of Zeus and Leto, and twin brother of Artemis. He was god of music, archery and prophecy. In the Trojan War he supported the Trojans.

ATHENA – Daughter of Zeus. She was born mature and fully armed from his head. She was goddess of handicraft, and protectress of many cities, but especially Athens. She was the embodiment of wisdom, and in the Trojan War she supported the Greeks.

CHIRON – A centaur, half-man, half-horse, who lived in a cave on Mt. Pelion. He was wise and kind, and learned in music and medicine. He taught Achilles the art of warfare, and how to run fast so he became the swiftest of the warriors on the battlefield.

ERIS – A minor goddess, and the personification of Strife and Discord.

HECTOR – Elder son of King Priam and Hecuba.

HECUBA – Wife of King Priam of Troy, and mother of Hector and Paris.

HELEN – Wife of King Menelaus. She was the daughter of Tyndareus, king of Sparta, and Leda. Although it is believed Zeus loved Leda and turned himself into a swan to seduce her, and Helen was really his daughter.

HEPHAESTUS – Lame son of Zeus and Hera. He excelled in metal work and made exquisite artefacts in gold and silver.

HERA – Wife of Zeus, goddess of women and marriage. She supported the Greeks in the Trojan War.

MENELAUS – Married to Helen. He became king of Sparta on his marriage. His brother was Agamemnon.

MYRMIDONS – Subjects of King Peleus. They fought under Achilles' command.

NEREIDS – Daughters of Nereus. Sea-deities.

NEREUS – A wise and kindly sea-deity, father of Thetis.

ODYSSEUS – Son of Laertes, king of Ithaka. One of the finest of the Greek heroes.

OENONE – A nymph on Mt. Ida, married to Paris.

PARIS – Son of King Priam of Troy and his wife Hecuba. He seduced Helen.

PELEUS – King of Phthia whose wife was Thetis. Their son was Achilles.

PRIAM – King of Troy, husband of Hecuba, and father of Hector and Paris.

THETIS – Daughter of Nereus. She married King Peleus and their son was Achilles.

TYNDAREUS – King of Sparta, mortal father of Helen.

ZEUS – Supreme god of the ancient world. He sometimes supported the Trojans, sometimes the Greeks in the Trojan War. In general he left it to the other gods to intervene in the war as they saw fit. He was said to be the father of Helen.

MORE FROM THE
PUT IT IN YOUR POCKET SERIES

GREEK ISLAND MYTHS

ALL YOU NEED TO KNOW ABOUT
THE ISLAND'S MYTHS, LEGENDS
AND ITS GODS

CHIOS

CRETE

KOS

NAXOS

RHODES

SANTORINI

ALSO BY JILL DUDLEY

YE GODS! (TRAVELS IN GREECE)
YE GODS! II (MORE TRAVELS IN GREECE)
LAP OF THE GODS (TRAVELS IN CRETE
AND THE AEGEAN ISLANDS)